Be, Happier

A JOURNAL

Pam Garramone, M.Ed.

Have you ever wished you could feel happier? Maybe your overall day-to-day feeling of happiness or contentment is a four or five out of ten and you'd like it to be a seven or eight more consistently; maybe most of the time you feel kind of blah or that things are okay but not great. The positive psychology practices in this journal will help you to increase your happiness. Experience what science proves: you can become happier by practicing happiness habits. For the last five years, I've kept a journal where every night before bed, I write three good things and five things for which I'm grateful. This practice has made me feel much happier and it can for you too.

Give it a try!

The Practice: Three good things

Every night, before you go to bed, write down at least three good things that have happened in the last 24 hours. You don't have to stop at three; it can be five, seven or more, but write at least three things. They can be small or big. It can be something that made you laugh, smile, feel proud or happy. It can be something you saw someone do that was kind. There really are no rules; you decide what was good and write it down.

For example, here's how I do it.

> **Three good things:** I made my 14 year old friend Dylan crack up laughing while playing darts! I finished everything on my to do list! I went for a long walk on the beach! *(you don't have to stop at three)* A friend sent me a super sweet email for Valentine's Day! NYC pizza and bagels!

To make this practice a habit, make it easier by keeping this journal and a pen next to your bed.

Three good things works because it changes our focus from what went wrong to what went well. Simply put, the more you look for good things, the more good things you start to see.

Five things I'm grateful for

Dr. Robert A. Emmons, University of California, Davis, Dr. Michael E. McCullough, University of Miami, and Dr. Martin E. P. Seligman, University of Pennsylvania, have done extensive research on the benefits of practicing gratitude.

These include feeling happier, more energetic, hopeful and helpful, empathetic, spiritual and religious, forgiving and optimistic. Studies show you're less likely to feel materialistic, lonely, neurotic, depressed and anxious.

The practice is to write five things you're grateful for each night. You can repeat similar things from other nights or not. Close your eyes, feel what comes up and then write it down.

I always include my health because to me that is most important. For example, here's how I do it.

Five things I'm grateful for:

I'm grateful for my health! I'm grateful for Leo [my dog] who greeted me with such joy and elation! I'm grateful for the delicious lunch at today's conference! I'm grateful to a stranger who complimented me on my hair! I'm grateful for the TV series, *This Is Us*, which moves me to tears every episode!

If you've ever kept a gratitude journal and didn't feel any happier, it's likely because you just wrote the same list every day without feeling any emotions. For example, I am grateful for my health, family, friends, job, home. Research indicates no increase in happiness from this kind of rote writing on your gratitude list. Instead, be specific and feel the feeling you had when it happened. Instead, "I'm so grateful I didn't get a ticket when I went overtime on the parking meter!".

Now you're ready! I hope these two positive psychology practices help you on your journey as you seek to *Be, Happier*.

POSITIVE PSYCHOLOGY SPEAKER
LIFE COACH

_____ / _____ /

Three good things:

_____

_____

_____

_____

_____

Five things I'm grateful for:

_____

_____

_____

_____

_____

_____

Three good things:

_____

_____

_____

_____

Five things I'm grateful for:

_____

_____

_____

_____

_____

_____

_____/_____/_____

Three good things:

_____

_____

_____

Five things I'm grateful for:

_____

_____

_____

_____

_____

Three good things:

_____

_____

_____

_____

Five things I'm grateful for:

_____

_____

_____

_____

_____

_____

_____ / _____ / _____

Three good things:

_____

_____

_____

_____

_____

Five things I'm grateful for:

_____

_____

_____

_____

_____

_____

Three good things:

_____

_____

_____

_____

Five things I'm grateful for:

_____

_____

_____

_____

_____

When we appreciate the good,

the good appreciates.

DR. TAL BEN-SHAHAR

Three good things:

_____

_____

_____

_____

Five things I'm grateful for:

_____

_____

_____

_____

_____

_____ / _____ / _____

Three good things:

_____

_____

_____

_____

Five things I'm grateful for:

_____

_____

_____

_____

_____

_____

Three good things:

_____

_____

_____

_____

Five things I'm grateful for:

_____

_____

_____

_____

_____

_____ / _____ / _____

Three good things:

_____

_____

_____

_____

Five things I'm grateful for:

_____

_____

_____

_____

_____

_____

Three good things:

_____

_____

_____

_____

Five things I'm grateful for:

_____

_____

_____

_____

_____

_____ / _____ / _____

Three good things:

_____

_____

_____

_____

Five things I'm grateful for:

_____

_____

_____

_____

_____

Make yourself feel good and make the people around you feel good and you will feel happier.

PAM GARRAMONE

_____ / _____ /

Three good things:

_____

_____

_____

_____

Five things I'm grateful for:

_____

_____

_____

_____

_____

_____

Three good things:

_____

_____

_____

_____

Five things I'm grateful for:

_____

_____

_____

_____

_____

_____

_____ / _____ / _____

Three good things:

_____

_____

_____

_____

Five things I'm grateful for:

_____

_____

_____

_____

_____

Three good things:

_____

_____

_____

_____

Five things I'm grateful for:

_____

_____

_____

_____

_____

_____ / _____ / _____

Three good things:

_____

_____

_____

_____

_____

Five things I'm grateful for:

_____

_____

_____

_____

_____

_____

Three good things:

_____

_____

_____

_____

_____

Five things I'm grateful for:

_____

_____

_____

_____

_____

_____

There are only two
ways to live your life.

One is
as though
nothing is
a miracle.

The other
is as though
everything
is a miracle.

ALBERT EINSTEIN

Three good things:

_____

_____

_____

_____

Five things I'm grateful for:

_____

_____

_____

_____

_____

_____

_____ / _____ / _____

Three good things:

_____

_____

_____

_____

_____

Five things I'm grateful for:

_____

_____

_____

_____

_____

_____

Three good things:

_____

_____

_____

_____

Five things I'm grateful for:

_____

_____

_____

_____

_____

_____

_____ / _____ / _____

Three good things:

_____

_____

_____

_____

Five things I'm grateful for:

_____

_____

_____

_____

_____

Three good things:

_____

_____

_____

_____

_____

Five things I'm grateful for:

_____

_____

_____

_____

_____

_____ / _____ / _____

Three good things:

_____

_____

_____

_____

_____

Five things I'm grateful for:

_____

_____

_____

_____

_____

_____

Your brain on positive performs significantly better than on negative, neutral or stressed.

SHAWN ACHOR

_____ / _____ / _____

Three good things:

_____

_____

_____

Five things I'm grateful for:

_____

_____

_____

_____

_____

Three good things:

_____

_____

_____

_____

Five things I'm grateful for:

_____

_____

_____

_____

_____

_____

_____ / _____ / _____

Three good things:

_____

_____

_____

_____

_____

Five things I'm grateful for:

_____

_____

_____

_____

_____

_____

Three good things:

_____

_____

_____

_____

_____

Five things I'm grateful for:

_____

_____

_____

_____

_____

_____

_____ / _____ / _____

Three good things:

_____

_____

_____

_____

Five things I'm grateful for:

_____

_____

_____

_____

_____

Three good things:

_____

_____

_____

_____

_____

Five things I'm grateful for:

_____

_____

_____

_____

_____

Imagine everyone has
an invisible sign hanging
from their neck saying

Make me feel
important.

Never forget this
message when working
with people.

MARY KAY ASH

/ /

Three good things:

Five things I'm grateful for:

_____ / _____ / _____

Three good things:

_____

_____

_____

_____

Five things I'm grateful for:

_____

_____

_____

_____

_____

Three good things:

_____

_____

_____

_____

_____

Five things I'm grateful for:

_____

_____

_____

_____

_____

_____

_____ / _____ / _____

Three good things:

_____

_____

_____

_____

Five things I'm grateful for:

_____

_____

_____

_____

_____

Three good things:

_____

_____

_____

_____

_____

Five things I'm grateful for:

_____

_____

_____

_____

_____

_____ / _____ / _____

Three good things:

_____

_____

_____

_____

_____

Five things I'm grateful for:

_____

_____

_____

_____

_____

_____

The brain is like Teflon for the good and Velcro for the bad.

DR. RICK HANSON

_____ / _____ / _____

Three good things:

_____

_____

_____

_____

_____

Five things I'm grateful for:

_____

_____

_____

_____

_____

_____

Three good things:

_____

_____

_____

_____

Five things I'm grateful for:

_____

_____

_____

_____

_____

_____ / _____ / _____

Three good things:

_____

_____

_____

_____

_____

Five things I'm grateful for:

_____

_____

_____

_____

_____

_____

Three good things:

_____

_____

_____

_____

Five things I'm grateful for:

_____

_____

_____

_____

_____

_____

_____ / _____ / _____

Three good things:

_____

_____

_____

_____

_____

Five things I'm grateful for:

_____

_____

_____

_____

_____

_____

/ /

Three good things:

Five things I'm grateful for:

Happiness depends upon ourselves.

ARISTOTLE

Three good things:

_____

_____

_____

_____

_____

Five things I'm grateful for:

_____

_____

_____

_____

_____

_____

_____ / _____ / _____

Three good things:

_____

_____

_____

_____

_____

Five things I'm grateful for:

_____

_____

_____

_____

_____

_____ / _____ / _____

Three good things:

_____

_____

_____

_____

_____

Five things I'm grateful for:

_____

_____

_____

_____

_____

_____

_____/_____/_____

Three good things:

_____

_____

_____

_____

_____

Five things I'm grateful for:

_____

_____

_____

_____

_____

_____

_____

_____ / _____ / _____

Three good things:

_____

_____

_____

_____

_____

Five things I'm grateful for:

_____

_____

_____

_____

_____

_____

_____ / _____ / _____

Three good things:

_____

_____

_____

_____

_____

Five things I'm grateful for:

_____

_____

_____

_____

_____

The more thankful
I became the more
my bounty increased.
That's because what
you focus on expands.

When you focus on
the goodness in
life, you create
more of it.

OPRAH WINFREY

_____ / _____ / _____

Three good things:

_____

_____

_____

_____

Five things I'm grateful for:

_____

_____

_____

_____

_____

_____

Three good things:

_____

_____

_____

_____

Five things I'm grateful for:

_____

_____

_____

_____

_____

_____ / _____ / _____

Three good things:

_____

_____

_____

_____

_____

Five things I'm grateful for:

_____

_____

_____

_____

_____

Three good things:

_____

_____

_____

_____

_____

Five things I'm grateful for:

_____

_____

_____

_____

_____

_____

_____/_____/_____

Three good things:

_____

_____

_____

_____

_____

Five things I'm grateful for:

_____

_____

_____

_____

_____

_____

Three good things:

_____

_____

_____

_____

_____

Five things I'm grateful for:

_____

_____

_____

_____

_____

Be happy for this moment. This moment is your life.

OMAR KHAYYAM

Three good things:

_____

_____

_____

_____

_____

Five things I'm grateful for:

_____

_____

_____

_____

_____

_____ / _____ / _____

Three good things:

_____

_____

_____

_____

_____

Five things I'm grateful for:

_____

_____

_____

_____

_____

Three good things:

_____

_____

_____

_____

_____

Five things I'm grateful for:

_____

_____

_____

_____

_____

_____

_____

_____ / _____ / _____

Three good things:

_____

_____

_____

_____

_____

Five things I'm grateful for:

_____

_____

_____

_____

_____

_____

Three good things:

_____

_____

_____

_____

_____

Five things I'm grateful for:

_____

_____

_____

_____

_____

_____

_____ / _____ / _____

Three good things:

_____

_____

_____

_____

Five things I'm grateful for:

_____

_____

_____

_____

_____

_____

When we
take time to
notice the things
that go right,
it means we're
getting a lot
of little rewards
throughout the day.

MARTIN SELIGMAN

_____ / _____ / _____

Three good things:

_____

_____

_____

_____

Five things I'm grateful for:

_____

_____

_____

_____

_____

Three good things:

_____

_____

_____

_____

Five things I'm grateful for:

_____

_____

_____

_____

_____

_____ / _____ / _____

Three good things:

_____

_____

_____

_____

Five things I'm grateful for:

_____

_____

_____

_____

_____

_____

Three good things:

_____

_____

_____

_____

_____

Five things I'm grateful for:

_____

_____

_____

_____

_____

_____

_____ / _____ / _____

Three good things:

_____

_____

_____

_____

_____

Five things I'm grateful for:

_____

_____

_____

_____

_____

_____

Three good things:

_____

_____

_____

_____

_____

Five things I'm grateful for:

_____

_____

_____

_____

_____

_____

_____

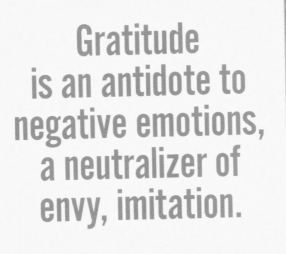

Gratitude
is an antidote to
negative emotions,
a neutralizer of
envy, imitation.

It is savoring;
it is not taking
things for granted;
it is present
oriented.

SONJA LYUBOMIRSKY

Three good things:

_____

_____

_____

_____

_____

Five things I'm grateful for:

_____

_____

_____

_____

_____

_____

_____ / _____ / _____

Three good things:

_____

_____

_____

_____

_____

Five things I'm grateful for:

_____

_____

_____

_____

_____

_____

Three good things:

_____

_____

_____

_____

_____

Five things I'm grateful for:

_____

_____

_____

_____

_____

_____

_____ / _____ / _____

Three good things:

_____

_____

_____

_____

_____

Five things I'm grateful for:

_____

_____

_____

_____

_____

Three good things:

_____

_____

_____

_____

_____

Five things I'm grateful for:

_____

_____

_____

_____

_____

_____

_____ / _____ / _____

Three good things:

_____

_____

_____

_____

Five things I'm grateful for:

_____

_____

_____

_____

_____

_____

_____ / _____ / _____

Three good things:

_____

_____

_____

_____

_____

Five things I'm grateful for:

_____

_____

_____

_____

_____

_____

_____

_____ / _____ / _____

Three good things:

_____

_____

_____

_____

_____

Five things I'm grateful for:

_____

_____

_____

_____

_____

_____

Not having the best situation but seeing the best in your situation is the key to happiness.

MARIE FORLEO

Notes

Notes

Notes